FOREX CURRENCY TRADING

All You Need to Know to Start Up a Profitable

Forex Trading Journey

Abraham Robert. C

In order to say thank you for purchasing this book, I offer the below video course and more to you as a token of appreciation

__Find the Link to the bonus video courses at the end of the book__

TABLE OF CONTENT

CHAPTER 1

INTRODCUTION TO CURRENCY TRADING

What Exactly Is Forex

The simultaneous purchase and sale of one currency for another is known as foreign exchange. Currencies are processed in currency pairs and exchanged through a broker or dealer.

With a daily turnover of over $5 trillion, the Foreign Exchange Market (FOREX) is the biggest financial market globally. This exceeds by over three times the aggregate value of the stock and futures markets put together. The FOREX spot market is devoid of a central exchange and physical presence, in contrast to other financial markets.

Through the electronic network of banks, businesses, and private individuals transferring one currency for another, it functions.

Because of its enormous turnover, forex trading is also the most well-liked financial market in the world today. Trading forex is the process of exchanging one currency for another at a predetermined exchange rate.

When trading a currency pair, such as AUD/USD, where you are speculating on AUD versus USD, traders will buy one while selling the other at the same time. In this case, if a trader believes that the value of the AUD would decline in relation to the USD, they will sell it. Conversely, if you believe that the value of AUD will increase relative to USD, you will purchase AUD and sell USD at the same time.

You will make some money if you were correct in the first two scenarios, but you will lose money if you were incorrect in one or both of the movements.

The forex market is open around-the-clock, covering many time zones in the main financial centers due to the absence of a physical exchange. Because it affects every facet of the FOREX experience, it is crucial to remember that there is no centralized exchange.

In this context, currency refers to any sort of money that is used as a medium of exchange. Currency values fluctuate in relation to one another, which is typically referred to as fluctuations in value inside the currency market. There are several elements which ascertain the amount that a specific currency will sell for in the market at a given time tempo.

Among these variables are the following that can affect the strength of a currency

- ✓ The monetary system
- ✓ Stability in politics and the economy
- ✓ Floods and earthquakes.
- ✓ Interference with currency
- ✓ War

Forex traders mostly concentrate on the deal since they want to make money from it. variations in the market value of one currency relative to another. To achieve this, they speculating on the probable future direction of the currency market's pricing. Money.

Prices are always changing in relation to one another; thus, this is an opportunity Traders seize opportunities to earn. Forex markets are typically available for business 24 hours a day, and this has made this exchange quite well-known. This market is now accessible to everyone, everywhere, and gives those with minimal financial resources the chance to earn some money.

In forex trading, currencies are exchanged in pairs—one currency against the other. In 90% of cases. The US dollar is the most traded currency in all of FX trading worldwide. It is is what you will utilize, whether you are buying or selling, in relation to another currency.

Think about the following scenario: USD/EUR or EUR/USD. These two are not the same. The commodity is the currency that shows up initially, and the one that The term "money" comes in second.

To engage in currency trading, you must register for a trading account with a forex trading advisor.

You have the option to select the currency you will use when you establish an account. would rather trade in. The most often used currencies are CAD, JPY, GBP, EUR, USD, and NZD, CHF, and AUD. The most liquid currencies are these ones. Although USD is used in practically all deals, EUR/JPY may also be used.

GBP/JPY and GBP/EUR. There are a lot of purchasers for these additional pairs, and vendors. You might be able to trade with a few other small currencies in the market for exchanging currencies. Rarely, but when macroeconomic events have an impact on certain currencies, there's a possibility of profit.

Among them are the Hong Kong currency, the Turkish lira, South African rand, Mexican peso, and Norwegian krone.

CHAPTER 2

FOREX PAIR

A pair of currencies that are traded against one another is known as a forex pair. While there are countless possible pairings, three of the most often used ones include the United States dollar vs the Japanese yen (USD/JPY), the British pound versus the United state dollar (GBP/USD), and the euro versus the US dollar (EUR/USD).

A quotation of two distinct currencies, one quoted against the other, is called a currency pair. Within a currency pair, the first stated currency is referred to as the base, and the second currency, which serves as the benchmark, is referred to as the quotation.

To find out how much of the quote currency is needed to purchase one unit of the base currency, currency pairings are supposed to be compared against one another. Each currency frequently has a three-letter sign attached to it In order to be identified. For example, the American dollar is classified as "USD" when it is represented in foreign markets.

The foreign exchange market involves a lot of trading in currency pairs. The foreign exchange market facilitates the purchase, sale, and conversion of currencies for trading and investment purposes globally.

Currency is constantly bought and sold in forex trading. Investors buy the base currency and sell the quoted currency when buying a currency pair. The quantity of quote currency required to get one unit of base currency is represented by the bid price.

In contrast, the investor sells the base currency and gets the quotation currency when they sell the currency pair. As a result, the amount one will get in the quote currency in exchange for one unit of the base currency is the selling price of the currency pair.

The Base and Quote Currency

In a currency pair, the quote is always on the right and the base currency is always on the left. The quote currency is equal to the current quotation price of the pair, which indicates how many of the quote currency will be needed to purchase one base. The base currency is always equal to one. Therefore, selling one currency to purchase another is a constant in currency trading.

Lot size

To standardize forex trading, currencies are traded in lots, or batches of currency. Because of the often-minor swings in foreign exchange prices, lots are typically relatively big. For instance, 100,000 units of the base currency make up a normal lot.

Lots, or essentially the number of currency units you will purchase or sell, are the particular sums used in forex trading. A quantity used to measure transactions is called a "lot." Order sizes are quoted in lots when you make orders on your trading platform. There are now mini, micro, and nano lot sizes that are 10,000, 1,000, and 100 units of money in addition to the traditional lot size of 100,000 units.

Major Currency Pairs

Major currency pairings are pairs of currencies that trade against the US dollar. These combinations are extremely popular and highly liquid since USD is the currency that is exchanged the most worldwide. Since large currency pairings have very modest spreads and are often the most predictable, novice traders will usually concentrate on them.

Specifically, the field of foreign exchange trading acknowledges a set of seven currency pairs referred to as the "major pairs," which comprise:

EUR/USD   USD/JPY   GBP/USD   USD/CHF   AUD/USD   USD/CAD   NZD/USD

Minor Currency Pairs

Minor currency pairs, often called "crosses," are trades between two large-cap currencies that exclude the US dollar. Minor currency pairs, as opposed to major currency pairs, consist of a major currency and a less well-liked or less liquid currency. This implies that small currency pairs have greater spreads than big currency pairs but are often less volatile.

Here are a few of the minor pairings that are most often traded:

EUR/GBP AUD/JPY EUR/CHF GBP/JPY

Minor currency pairings can provide traders with a chance to diversify their holdings and benefit from various market circumstances across national borders. Because of their greater spreads and lower liquidity than big currency pairings, they can also be riskier.

Forex Pip

In forex trading, a pip is a unit of measurement used to express the difference in value between two currencies. Pip, which stands for "point in percentage," is the lowest standard deviation that may be made in a monetary quote. Traders use pip values to indicate the profit or loss on their position and to compute the difference between the ask and bid prices of a currency pair.

A pip is defined as the fourth decimal place in the majority of major currencies; hence one pip is equal to 0.0001. However, there are few outliers, like the Japanese Yen, in which the digit that comes after the decimal point is called a pip. Despite the fact that a pip is often the second or fourth decimal place, we frequently show a fraction of a pip as an extra decimal.

Since the spread in a currency pair is a measurement of the shift in market prices, it may be stated in pip values. You may think of a pip as the movement's "point" equivalent.

Leverage

Traders utilize leverage as a strategy to control a significant amount of capital with a much smaller initial deposit. With leveraged trading, you just need to put up a lesser amount known as margin, as opposed to traditional investing where you have to tie up the entire value of your position. For instance, with 25:1 leverage, you can control $25 of a stake with $1

Because they don't want to commit a lot of money to every deal, more retail traders are now able to access markets like forex thanks to leverage. It should be utilized carefully though, since it will amplify both the gains and losses from every deal.

Margin

Trading on margin is an option available to players in the Forex market. One of the alluring and riskiest aspects of forex trading is the option to trade on margin. In essence, margin trading enables forex traders to make trades using borrowed money.

The trader's ability to borrow money will be influenced by the broker they choose and the leverage or gearing they provide.

In trading, margin is the amount of money needed to initiate and keep a position. When you trade on margin, you only need to put up a small portion of a deal's total value to gain full market exposure. Usually, the necessary margin requirement is expressed as a percentage.

The way margin trading operates is that it allows you to initiate a trade with a little initial commitment. Your trading provider's margin system will decide the margin, and the asset being traded will determine how much cash is needed. A greater deposit can be necessary for those with more volatility or larger investments.

When trading, there are two kinds of margin to take into account: initial margin and maintenance margin. Often referred to as the deposit margin or simply the deposit, the initial margin is the amount needed to initiate the position. The amount of money required in your account to fund the position's present value and offset any running losses is known as maintenance margin.

Spread

In essence, it is the difference between the prices you pay to purchase and sell the assets you are currently trading.

Depending on what your broker is offering, the way the spread operates in forex will vary slightly. Generally speaking, fixed and variable spreads are the two basic varieties you may encounter.

Irrespective of volatility, a fixed spread is constant.

Variable spreads are more common among providers that pass on third-party pricing, whereas fixed spreads are offered by providers that function as market makers themselves, acting as a counterparty to their clients' trades. A variable spread can tighten and loosen with volatility to account for different levels of risk.

Variable spreads have the potential to be less expensive under more stable market conditions, while fixed spreads are advantageous in times of high volatility when spreads usually widen.

Because they can be pretty certain of the price they will pay and the expenses they will incur, some forex traders prefer fixed spreads. Slippage, which occurs when the market moves swiftly and the price fluctuates between the level you place your order at and the price your broker can execute at, can affect even fixed spreads.

In the forex market, the spread cost is determined by the state of the market and the terms of your broker's agreement, such as whether you have variable or fixed spreads.

Assuming a variable spread, trading expenses grow during erratic markets to cover your broker's higher risk and decrease during stable markets.

While a variety of variables can cause volatility, in the foreign exchange market, the biggest culprits are the releases of economic data and breaking news. Because of this, it's critical to keep track of dates in an economic calendar in order to determine whether impending events might have an impact on the currency pair you're trading.

The spread's price is also influenced by the Forex pair you select. Because they have less liquidity than major currency pairs, emerging market and economy currency pairings usually have a wider range.

Bid Price

In the foreign exchange market, the bid is the price at which the market is willing to purchase a certain currency pair.

The desired price is chosen by the buying merchant. This is the highest amount that a buyer is willing to pay to purchase an asset, also known as the bid price. The law of supply and demand dictates that the customer does not want to purchase pricey goods.

Ask Price

In the foreign exchange market, the ask is the price at which the market is willing to sell a certain currency pair. The ask price is determined by the merchant who sells.

The lowest price at which the seller is willing to sell a security is known as the "ask price," also known as the offer price. The vendor would like to sell it for more money.

Ask and Bid Price

The seller raises the Ask price when there are good grounds to do so for an asset. As a result, the buyer decides to increase the bid price after realizing that there is little possibility to acquire the asset at the previous price.

The procedure is reversed when an asset's price drops. The seller is compelled to reevaluate their expectations from the deal and lower the Ask price, while the buyer lowers the Bid price in an effort to purchase the item at a lower cost.

A transaction happens when the seller agrees to sell the asset right away to a buyer at the price they desire, or when the seller finds a buyer willing to pay the seller the price they want for the item.

CHAPTER 3

THE BULL MARKET

A bull market is characterized by a high level of market confidence, a majority of investors purchasing, and rising prices. In a particular market, if prices rise quickly, this might indicate that most investors are growing more confident, or "bullish," about future price increases, and could indicate that a bull market is about to begin.

A bull market makes consumers feel positive about investing. Because they anticipate more growth and bigger returns, buyers are acting more aggressively as a result of the strong level of investor confidence. This increasing momentum is usually driven by positive economic data and predictions of future expansion.

The possibility that forex trading presents to traders in both bull and bear markets is one of its main advantages. This is due to the fact that forex trading is usually done in pairs, so you may profit from rising and falling markets when one currency weakens and the other strengthens.

It is crucial to monitor bull and bear markets as they might reveal trends in the currency market. Knowing the current state of the market can assist you in managing risk and determining the ideal times to enter and exit transactions.

When prices are rising in a bull market, traders want to enter the market so they may sell when they think the market has peaked.

The extremes of the emotion spectrum are represented by "fear" and "greed," with bull markets attracting investors eager to get in on the latest trend and bear markets attracting short sellers eager to profit from plunging prices. When these indicators reach extreme levels, they may also portend a turning point in the market since excessively one-sided positioning leaves the trend open to reversal.

The words "bear market" and "bull market" refer to the general trend of a financial market. When the nation has an economic downturn, such as a recession or an increase in unemployment, it becomes more difficult to keep stock values growing. This causes investors to feel fearful and discourages them from taking on riskier investments.

There are a number of reasons why a bull market might turn into a bear market:

Overvaluation: Bull markets frequently have an exuberant period of optimism and investor euphoria, which causes assets to be overvalued. A correction or reversal in market sentiment may occur when prices reach unsustainable levels, which might result in a bear market.

Shifts in the economy: such as inflationary pressures, increasing interest rates, slower economic development, or geopolitical concerns, can cause investor confidence to decline and turn a bull market into a bear market.

Economic factors: A change in the economy, whether it be due to a slowdown in growth, an increase in interest rates, inflationary pressures, or geopolitical concerns, can cause investor confidence to decline and turn a bull market into a bear market.

Market psychology: The mood of the market and the psychology of investors influence the path the market follows. Investors may act in unison during a bull market, pushing prices higher. On the other hand, negative emotion brought on by panic, fear, or uncertainty can cause the market to move quickly in the wrong direction and usher in a bear market.

A bear market, on the other hand, may emerge if sentiment quickly shifts negative as a consequence of anxiety, fear, or panic.

Corporate profits: Robust increase in corporate earnings has been known to bolster bull markets. But if businesses start releasing bad news about their outlooks, weakening fundamentals, or disappointing results, it can erode investor confidence and lead the market to turn bearish.

On the other hand, it can erode investor confidence and contribute to a move towards a bear market if corporations start to announce disappointing profits, worsening fundamentals, or poor outlooks.

Changes in regulations, central bank activities, or government policies can all have an effect on market dynamics. Monetary policy changes, such raising interest rates or decreasing liquidity, can have an impact on borrowing costs, company investment, and consumer spending. They may also cause the market to turn from bullish to bearish.

Monetary policy changes, including interest rate tightening or decreased liquidity, can impact consumer spending, company investment, and borrowing prices. These changes may even cause the market to turn from bull to bear.

External occurrences: Markets can be disrupted and sentiment can change by way of unanticipated events like natural catastrophes, political unrest, or significant geopolitical wars.

CHAPTER 4

THE BEAR MARKET

A bear market is a period of economic contraction that may cause significant declines in the values of stocks, foreign exchange pairs, commodities, and other financial assets. This happens when there is a high percentage of unemployment, a decline in wages, a large number of individuals leaving the labor market, or decreased business earnings as a result of increasing competition.

A bear market is marked by declining prices, pessimistic mood, and typically a deteriorating economic environment. While bear markets tend to emerge faster than their counterparts, they can nonetheless cause severe price fluctuations and moves that might endure for months or years.

In a bull market, traders are ready to trade or invest and maintain positions for extended periods of time because they are confident in the state of the market. In a bear market, traders are always concerned about prices dropping because of the uncertainty that permeates the market. Because of the overwhelming uncertainty and dread of a sudden and severe reversal, it can be challenging to maintain your position and your nerve if you are short in a bear market. Because of the unpredictable price activity, traders may be persuaded to purchase and sell at levels they would not typically consider, which increases market volatility.

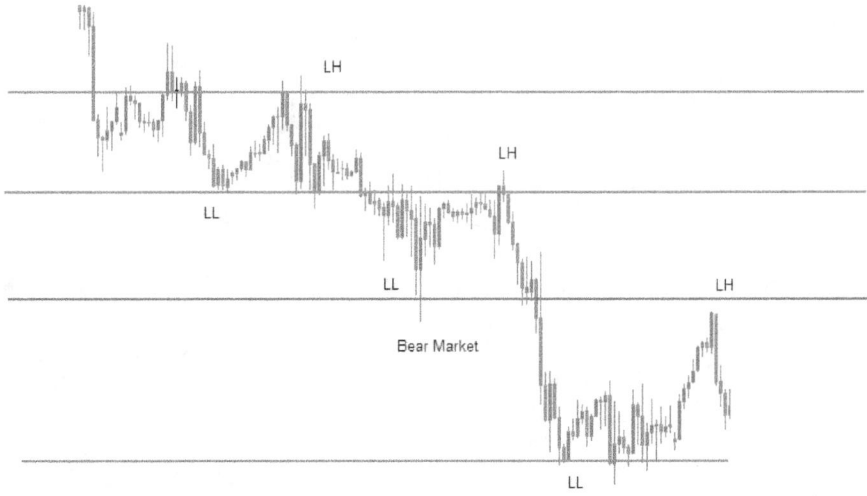

Large price declines can also encourage investors to enter the market again by encouraging them to " Purchase the dip." These investors then immediately liquidate their position as prices continue to decline, which exacerbates the negative mood and unpredictable price movement.

Bear markets typically produce a generalized sense of pessimism among investors since declining prices frequently translate into lower investment returns. Notwithstanding the declining prices and the general negative feeling, there are situations where investors might profit from bear markets.

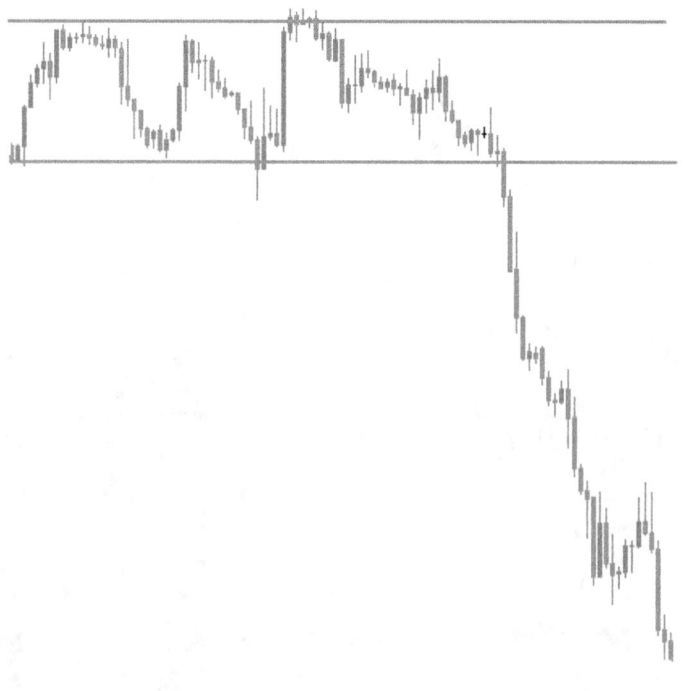

A person who is bearish is one who has negative expectations for the financial markets and the economy.

Such a person would often anticipate a decline in the value of a financial security as well as a downtrend.

Selling on pullbacks, or when prices climb higher in the near term, is a typical tactic used by pessimistic traders who believe that prices will soon begin to decline once more.

If you have a pessimistic outlook for the market, you anticipate price declines in the near future.

A scenario like this indicates a long-term declining tendency in the market. The asset values are either declining or are anticipated to deteriorate in the near future due to the negative outlook of the markets. As all securities prices decline, investors will lose a great deal of money, and a decline in investor confidence is also anticipated.

A bear market's traits and origins will change depending on the situation. Nonetheless, the projected course and duration are heavily influenced by market mood and economic cycles.

The following are a few signs of a faltering economy: Limited job possibilities, diminished Available funds for the general public to use, declining revenue for businesses, unprecedented adjustments to different tax rates or government rates etc.

CHAPTER 5

CHANGE IN MARKET DIRECTION

Events occurring throughout the world have a greater influence on forex than ever before due to the global engagement in foreign currency trading.

Some of the elements and trends influencing changes in the market are listed below.

Factors That Can Trigger A Change In Market Direction

News on Politics

The political climate has an impact on a nation's economics. The value of the currency is impacted in turn. Forex traders keep an eye on political developments and news to determine how they may impact other nations' economic policies. For instance, they can examine the amount of money spent by the government or the new laws and rules put in place for specific companies or sectors. Furthermore, modifications to the rules governing the leverage or margin that traders can use can have a significant effect on the markets.

Deflation

It is important to note that inflation may have an influence on the modifications. When a country experiences inflation, the value of money fluctuates periodically. Assume, for instance, that the inflation rate of one nation is lower than that of another. If that's the case, the value of that nation's currency will increase, requiring more of it to be purchased goods. In contrast, let's say that the rate of inflation in one nation is higher than in another. In that scenario, the nation's currency will depreciate (i.e., consumers will require less of it to purchase goods), and interest rates may rise.

Trade and Capital Balances

The movement of money into and out of nations causes the FX market to fluctuate regularly. For instance, a nation's currency would depreciate if its exports are reduced and it is largely dependent on them. Likewise, if investors transfer their funds within or across countries, it may signal a shift in public opinion.

Economic Shifts

The activity of any financial market is correlated with the economic stability of a nation. Statistical measures such as the gross domestic product are used to assess the overall health and performance of a nation's economy. This gauges the rate at which the economy is expanding or contracting. An economy in good shape is typically accompanied by a stronger currency as foreign investors seek to place their money there. This occurs as a result of the requirement for merchants to utilize local currency when purchasing financial assets within a nation.

National Debt

Countries can borrow money to invest in their economic growth by taking on public debt, which can raise living standards and promote consumer spending. On the other hand, excessive government debt can result in higher interest rates and more costly economic growth. Therefore, maintaining low interest rates while simultaneously strengthening the economy is necessary for a robust economy. It will also contribute to the stability of the national currency.

Conditions of Sale

The link between import and export prices is measured by the word trade. If the percentage is greater than 100%, then more capital is entering the nation than is leaving it, and if it is less than 100%, then more money is leaving the nation than is entering it. The phrase can assess the state of the economy and forecast the effects of foreign currency markets.

Rumor

You need to consider other potential influencing elements in order to estimate the currency rate's future fluctuations. For instance, expectations of rising exchange rates may lead other investors to place higher demands for the currency. You must exercise caution, though, and make sure you don't follow this trend too late.

CHAPTER 6

MAKING THE TRADE

Orders

An order is a directive to your broker, either now or in the future, to execute a certain trade in the market within predetermined criteria. An order can be carried out immediately or in the future. Pending orders require certain pricing behaviors before they may be executed immediately. A market order is intended to be executed right away at the best price your broker is willing to provide you.

The range of currency trading orders that broker-dealers accept has significantly increased in the last several years, both in terms of quantity and kind. Competition and customer desire for increased flexibility and trade execution alternatives have been the primary motivators. Market makers in particular, who handle their books better with a wide variety of orders, are glad to comply.

Orders can be further divided into three main functional types.

Market (Immediate Execution)

Limit (Pending Execution)

Stop (Pending Execution)

Market (Immediate Execution)

Market orders, sometimes referred to as quick executions, are the most prevalent sort of order. As the name suggests, the trader's buy or sell position is immediately carried out at the market price as it is at that moment. The order is made and automatically looks for the best price in the market to execute it at, depending on the broker selected.

With instant executions, dealers may trade at the given price, which is quite helpful. Do be aware of the volatility of the Forex market, as it may lead to abrupt price fluctuations. As a result, there will be times when the marker order is executed at a price that differs significantly from what was planned.

Limit (Pending Execution)

Most traders who want to make the sharpest entrance possible employ limit orders. Since a limit order would only be opened in the event that the predetermined limit order price was met, limit orders also do not necessitate continuous monitoring of the financial markets.

If a trader's chosen level is not reached, the limit order will not be filled; instead, it will not be executed until the desired level is reached.

Traders would not pay a cent extra for the order, but it may be completed at a price lower than the predetermined threshold. This is in contrast to instant execution, where the deal is live from the time traders purchase or sell.

Buy Limit Price

Buy Limit

Stop (Pending Execution)

Because stop orders are always executed in the direction that the market moves, traders typically use them to further check that the markets are moving in their favor before starting a transaction. Stop order users aim to enter the market only after prices have reached the buy stop price or exit the market only after prices have dropped to the sell stop price.

Entry Point

The price or level at which a trader initiates a trade (buy or sell) in forex is known as the entry point.

Because there are so many unpredictable variables influencing the forex market, a trader may find it challenging to choose when to enter the market.

Candlestick as A Point of Entry

Candlestick patterns are useful tools used by forex traders to determine entry points and alerts. Proficient traders frequently employ patterns such as the engulfing, hammer, morning and evening star, shooting star, and so on.

Evening Star Sell Signal

Morning Star Buy Signal

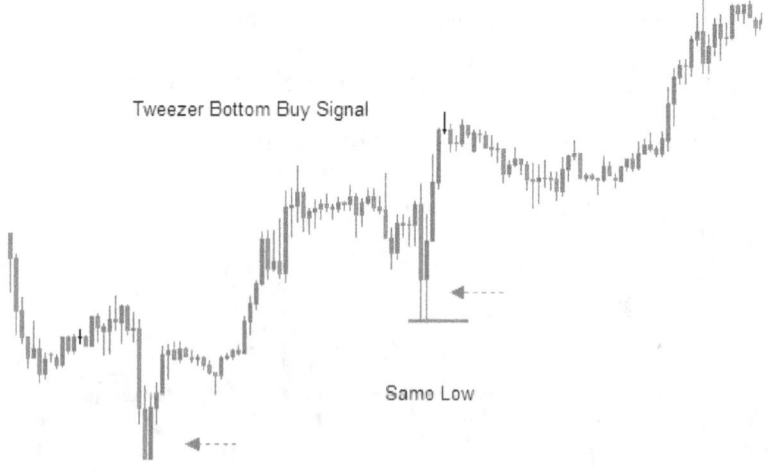

Tweezer Bottom Buy Signal

Samo Low

Breakouts Point of Entrance

Using breakouts as entry signals is one of the most often used trade entry tactics by traders. Finding important levels and taking advantage of them as trade entry points is known as breakout trading. Effective breakout methods require an understanding of price movement. The key component of breakout trading is when forex prices breach a predetermined level of support or resistance

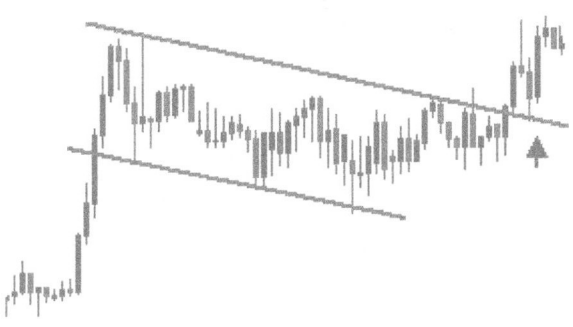

ss

Trend Channels Point of Entry

Trendlines are a fundamental tool used by technical analysts to determine regions of resistance and support. As price breaks through these critical levels of support and resistance, traders should be on the lookout for a potential breakout or trend reversal.

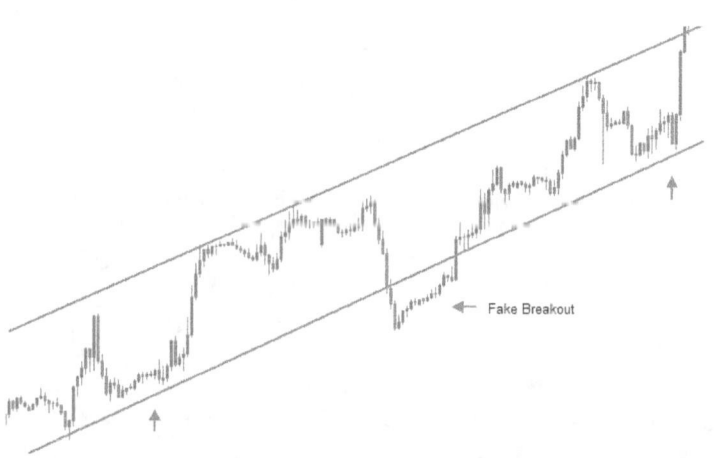

GET INSTANT ACCESS TO THE FREE VIDEO COURSE BY FOLLOWING THE BELOW LINK

subscribepage.io/freeforexcourse

Click or copy and paste the above link on your browser for instant access to the bonus video.

Happy Trading!

www.ingramcontent.com/pod-product-compliance
Lightning Source LLC
Chambersburg PA
CBHW062301290526
45794CB00006B/2643